Thank you for the help and support from my friends and family, and the love for food they increased in me. - A.A.M

To the little one who has given me a second chance at first experiences. - O.E.

First published in 2022 by Formy Books
International House
12 Constance Street
London E16 2DQ
formybooks.com

Designer: Curtis Ackie
Editor: Lauren Ackie

ISBN 978 1 8383959 3 3

1 2 22 22

British Library Cataloguing in Publication Data available.

ZAZI FINDS PLANTAIN

OGAGA EMUVEYAN

ASMA ADEN MOHAMED

est. 2020
Formy Books

Tonight we're going to have a big dinner,
but we're missing one thing.
So we're off to the market to buy some plantain!

It's my favourite food in all the world,
it's perfect with every main.

There's no better side for your dish
than juicy, sweet plantain!

We'll start looking over there,

there must be plantain here somewhere.

We'll check every stall, high and low,
until we find the platanos.

Hey Mr Tran!

We see you've got fresh vegetables
and crates full to the brim,
but really we were hoping that you've got
some ripe plantain!

Sorry my friends,
there's no plantain here,
but I do have this juicy
mango you could eat.

It's great in salads but on its own it's juicy and so sweet!

We'll keep looking over there,
there must be plantain here somewhere.

We'll check every stall, high and low,
until we find the platanos.

Hey Mrs Farzan,

We've got mangoes
but still we're missing something grand,
we wonder if perhaps you have some plantain at your stand?

Hey Zazi girl,
I'm sorry to say
I have nothing by that name.

But you're welcome to try this box of dates,
they're sweet and wonderful all the same.

We'll keep looking over there,
There must be plantain here somewhere.

We'll check every stall, high and low,
until we find the platanos.

Hi Miss Mensah!

We hope you can help.

We've got mangoes and dates
but we need something else,
do you have any plantain?

Oh no Zazi, I've sold my last one!
But here, have some okra,
they're slimy but yum!

We'll keep looking over there,
There must be plantain here somewhere.

We'll check every stall, high and low,
until we find the platanos.

Hey Mr Ellington,
here's the thing:

We've got mangoes, dates and okra,
but still no plantain!

Zazi you're in luck, I've got plenty of those,
come, take your pick from these delicious platanos!
We've got yellow and ripe, green and unripe too,
All you can eat, for Papa and you!

In our local market we found what we were looking for.

Our friends gave us what we needed and more.

We've got mangoes, dates, okra
and juicy sweet plantain.
Everything looks yummy,
so Papa let's tuck in!

Also available from Formy Books

est. 2020
Formy
Books